Nightworks

Note from the Composer

I recently recorded *Nightworks* on my solo piano album *Don't Say Goodbye* (CD1043). *Nightworks* was first published in 1993. Now available from FJH, it continues to captivate listeners and performers alike with its atmospheric, jazz-influenced style.

Edwin McLean

FJH2158

Contents

First Star

Edwin McLean

Moonlight Tonight

tricky rhythms

Nightfall

Serenade

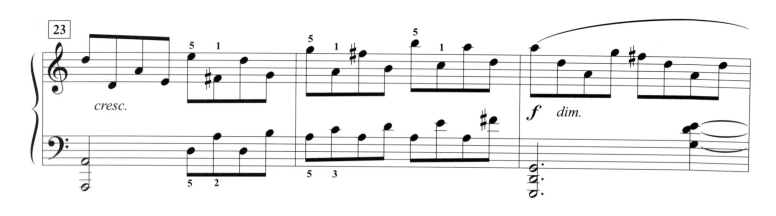

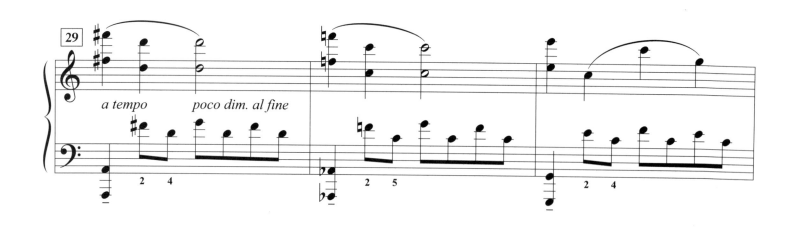

Fire and Shadows

Flowing (♩ = 148)

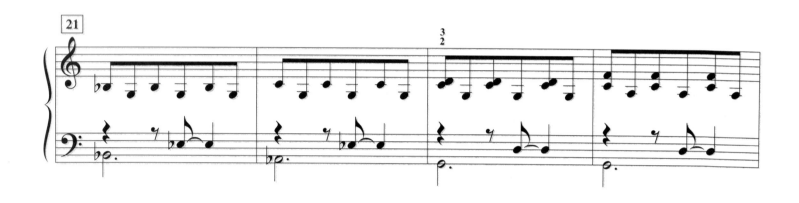

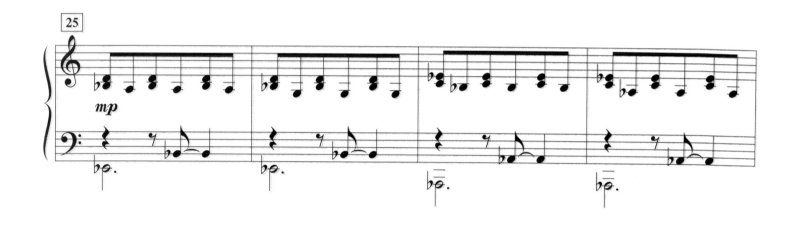

Daybreak